"Being faithful means giving your all to one person, both emotionally and physically."-
Unknown

Men, One Woman is Enough For You

WINSTON PECCOO

MEN, ONE WOMAN IS ENOUGH FOR YOU

Copyright ©2023 Winston Peccoo

Published by:

REASON
WITH ROBDON

ISBN: 978-1-990266-49-2

Scripture references are taken from the King James Version of the Bible.

All Emphasis in scripture quotations were added by the author.

Contact Reason Publishers at reasonwithrobdon@gmail.com

Cover design by: Iconic Presence

FOREWORD

Bishop Valentine Rodney

*Minister and Author, Church of God of Prophecy &
Word Impact Ministries*

Rev Winston Peccoo in his debut publication is fearless in continuing the conversation concerning relationship and the God intended model of having one partner. Many have hinted that monogamy is simply unrealistic being out of touch with today's realities. He is however undaunted in boldly sharing his view borne out of a longstanding conviction that is entrenched in his faith in God and the Bible. His frequent discussions into the areas of relationship on many platforms have earned him the title of the "love doctor" as he continuously offers relationship advice to countless others. This book with its bold assertion goes against the grain of speculation and the usual contempt held for such a noble position. He uses as the standard for the discussion the biblical manuscript, for who better to define the parameters of marriage but God who instituted it. He asserts that faith and trust are fundamental to marital faithfulness with one person and that you don't need multiple partners but multiple ways to please and commit to one partner. He posits the argument that soundness and wholeness in relationship is based on many parameters and not just restricted to sex. Rev Peccoo is not oblivious to the challenges that such a position holds. But asserts that fidelity is not only possible and commendable but is representative of the ideal.

This book is directed at men and is a clarion call to responsible action. He uses a plethora of vivid examples to demonstrate the deleterious effects of having multiple partners and the virtues of celebrating and living with one. Temptations are never a valid excuse to forego the biblical ideal or model. Every man is built and wired with the ability to resist and say no to them. It must be done not just because of the dangers posed but out of reverence for an eternal God. Resisting Rev. Peccoo admonishes may be challenging but not impossible. Every man faces temptations but need not succumb to its pressures to violate biblical standards.

This book will challenge you to rethink your position on infidelity and bring your passions and thought life in line with God and the scriptures which are the supreme architect of interpersonal relationships. Be prepared to add your voice and life to this vibrant and ever unfolding conversation.

ENDORSEMENT #1

Trinel Lyn

Marriage Coordinator – Positive Vibration 365+

Global

Research has shown that almost 90% of the world's population now live in countries with falling marriage rates. Two in five young adults perceive marriage as outdated and irrelevant. In an over-sexualised society, it is evident why some of these statistics are so prevalent as more couples, dating or in long-term relationships, are open to the many options available to their relationship to avoid 'boredom' or to 'add adventure'. The Macho Culture is still a powerful influence on the lives of our men, and with easy access to the explicit lyrics coming from the music industry whilst women are being presented as sex symbols seen on television and in magazines, the desire to be polygamous has become almost irresistible. Many couples, including married couples, are bold about their open relationship in the name of freedom and expression. Orgies, swingers, and the desire to be watched in promiscuous activities have become some of the goals many couples have today.

Regardless of the era we are encountering, God's word is timeless and applicable to all generations. Therefore, marriage is God's design, and a man should pursue one woman. Amidst the lies and false ideation of pleasure through these immoral acts, the intertwining of mind, body, and soul between one man and woman is more beautiful and permanently rewarding than any quick fix any licentious activities may offer. The aspiration to become a lifelong learner of your spouse's attitude, body and rhythm and the commitment to remain pure and honest to that special person signifies a strong sense of maturity, self-control, and the humility to trust God to help you learn, achieve, and grow in your union.

'Men, One Woman is Enough' is the ideal book that will shed some truths on the significance of honouring a monogamous relationship (marriage). The content of this powerful book is written with you in mind. It is enlightening, relevant and refreshing coming from another brother's perspective. A kingdom with too many queens will crumble but a man who leaves his father and mother to cleave to his woman and the two becoming flesh has the potential to build a kingdom with a lasting foundation. Why waste it on many when you can secure and multiply with one?

ENDORSEMENT #2

Rev Nicholas Robertson

Marriage Counselor – Positive Vibration 365+ Global

In a world where carnality is celebrated, and immorality is embraced, the book "Men, One Woman is Enough," written by Rev Winston Peccoo, is a resourceful tool that will empower men to recognise their worth, value women, and enjoy more fulfilling marriages The writer makes the case that having one woman allows for more fulfilling marriages The most obvious way to end a marriage is infidelity Men are encouraged and given practical to remain focused their marriages, love, cherish, and celebrate their wives Being faithful gives peace of mind as you don't have to watch your tracks, nor be paranoid, trying to remember every lie told The writer insinuates that having one woman will boost the quality of your sex life When your spouse knows you are faithful, your spouse will give you great sex; no one feels safe sexing a spouse who has been with another A man focused on his marriage learns to flirt and play with his spouse, creating greater orgasmic encounters and happier wives Several techniques are suggested to enhance playfulness in marriage Being faithful has a positive effect on your character That way, you can live out your greatness with confidence Integrity is important, and it starts with how you live your private life; it gives moral authority Faithful people are happier, more relaxed, and more fulfilled; they smile more; their conscience is clear, and they live a life that is not stressful, empty, or complicated Being faithful makes you proud of yourself Being faithful makes your wife trust you, and with trust, she surrenders and gives all to you, allowing you to get to know her deeply Without trust, you will never fully gain access to her heart

This book provides so much knowledge critical for thriving marriages. While it is written with men in mind, it is suitable for all people. It will help wives to support their spouses, mothers to guide their children, and boys to grow up and become faithful. Without any hesitation, I fully endorse this book as a tool necessary for all.

ENDORSEMENT #3

Danielle Brown-Robertson

Marriage Counsellor and Relationship Coach-Couples Corner, Positive Vibration 365+Global

Rev Winston Peccoo is an astute relationship guru from which he earned the name Dr Love. In this amazing book, "men, one woman is enough" he speaks to importance of fidelity in marriage which becomes possible when there is contentment and a deep reverence for God. With his experience in marriage and counselling over the years, he explores a plethora of ideas and approaches to fulfilling the fundamental purpose of marriage while enjoying the union and not merely enduring each other's involvement. While it may be directed to men, it is a tool that women can also find useful.

ACKNOWLEDGEMENT

Thanks to my wife Dian, Rev Nicholas Robertson, Rev Darren Mckoy, all my students, and social media followers who insistently encourage me to write a book and not just post small snippets on Facebook. You were integral in the successful completion of this milestone.

Special thanks to Mrs. Trinel Lyn, Mrs. Danielle Brown-Robertson (Mrs. Robdon), and Rev Nicholas Robertson for endorsing this masterpiece. Your words carefully sum up the intent.

Finally, thanks to Bishop Valentine Rodney for clinically documenting the foreword. You have meticulously introduced this work to all readers. The book is finally here. Let us engage!

TABLE OF CONTENTS

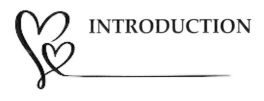 **INTRODUCTION**

Over the past several decades, our civilization has experimented with several alternatives to faithful marriage. Yet the evidence is abundant that from a personal as well as a public perspective, we are most likely to flourish when faithful, monogamous, natural-law marriages are plentiful and the norm.

In contemporary language, the concept of marital fidelity often boils down to refraining from engaging in sexual relations with anyone other than one's spouse. However, this narrow perspective not only oversimplifies the matter but also fixates excessively on the sexual dimension of marriage. If we align with the teachings of natural law, which define marriage as the sacred bond between a man and a woman who: 1) wholeheartedly give themselves to each other in mind, will, heart, and body; 2) embrace the potential for procreation; 3) commit to a lifelong partnership; and 4) remain exclusive (without any involvement of third parties), then the essence of fidelity extends beyond mere physical boundaries. It fundamentally revolves around remaining true to the profound exchange of selves that takes place within the institution of marriage. Over the years all of this has been eroded not just by people being polygamous but with them being polyamorous.

Hence, we can categorize various forms of betrayal that infringe upon distinct aspects of the marital union. A breach of fidelity in terms of intellect and will encompasses desiring or longing for emotional intimacy with someone outside the marital bond, which can even encompass neglecting one's spouse's needs without external involvement. Emotional infidelity, conversely, entails diverting one's emotional affections towards another person and neglecting the emotional requirements of one's spouse. And, naturally, physical infidelity involves the body and encompasses yielding to external physical, including sexual, interactions and/or disregarding the physical and sexual needs of one's spouse.

Essentially, the transgression of marital trust can manifest not only through sexual acts but also through various other means, such as forming intellectual or emotional connections with a friend of the opposite sex other than one's spouse.

In fact, intellectual and emotional unfaithfulness often serve as the steppingstones that pave the way for descending into sexual infidelity. Our existence is an intertwined harmony of body and soul, and the communion of our souls (through our thoughts and emotions) organically progresses to the unity of our physical forms. Consequently, safeguarding the sanctity of marital love entails channelling our most intimate treasures exclusively towards our spouse and repelling any alternative allurements.

THE PAIN OF IRREPRESSIBLE DESIRE

Occasionally, I encounter groups of unmarried and married men who assert that they cannot remain faithful to a single spouse. They use the analogy that committing to one woman for a lifetime is akin to condemning oneself to a monotonous diet. While this notion may appear humorous, it carries a more serious undertone.

Regrettably, many men lack a comprehensive understanding of the true essence and implications of marriage. It doesn't surprise me when some individuals express such sentiments; it reflects a lack of insight and spiritual awareness.

Marriage signifies a lifelong devotion to one's partner. It isn't about indulging in sexual experimentation with multiple individuals. Marriage marks the end of sexual recklessness. According to divine standards, entering marriage as a virgin is ideal. Yet, for those who have lost their virginity, they aren't abandoned by God. Instead, they are called to lead a virtuous sexual life thereafter. It's important to note that genuine emotional intimacy and affectionate communication are integral to a meaningful sexual relationship; without these, engaging in sexual activities with one's spouse could become akin to a form of domestic violation.

While sex is undoubtedly pleasurable, it's the responsibility of spouses to infuse their sexual life with excitement, adventure, and romance. Sex should never be mundane or uninviting; it ought to be an eagerly anticipated aspect of the relationship.

There is nothing alluring or admirable about a married man engaging in extramarital affairs. It exemplifies a severe lack of sexual responsibility and spiritual commitment.

The truth is, there is no sexual desire that a husband cannot fulfill within his marriage. A single wife offers a multitude of diverse experiences, much like a varied menu of culinary delights—ranging from chicken done in 101 different ways, stew peas, fish in blanket, pepper pot soup, and ice cream with various flavors. Viewing sex as a delicacy, one should recognize that a wife possesses the capacity to satisfy all such cravings. It's a matter of adjusting one's mindset and treating her with the appropriate attitude.

Dear men, every woman possesses unique qualities that may be appealing, until the point where desire for intimacy takes over. This could be physical attributes such as breasts, hips, lips, complexion, or voice. Constantly seeking new partners in the pursuit of these attractions will lead to an insatiable craving, much like attempting to consume an entire buffet of foods — ultimately resulting in discomfort.

Similarly, just as indulging in a variety of wines leads to a lack of appreciation, finding contentment with one preferred option yields the most genuine enjoyment. Remaining faithful isn't solely about your partner; it's a reflection of your personal commitment and character as a man.

The decision to remain loyal rests upon you, as does the responsibility to treat your partner like royalty.

A kingdom with multiple queens is unstable and destined to crumble. Loving one woman in countless ways is a true mark of greatness, far superior to a shallow affection for numerous women. The joy derived from faithfulness is immeasurable; dedicating your heart to one woman above all others is profoundly fulfilling.

Just as a rolling stone gathers no moss, a man who continually shifts from one woman to another never finds authentic happiness in life.

Fidelity dwells not in the domain of the fairer sex but resides deeply within your essence as a man. The choice to remain loyal rests squarely upon your shoulders, a testament to your commitment to the woman you hold dear. Amidst the kaleidoscope of feminine allure, there always exists a feature worthy of admiration, an ember of desire that might tempt you astray from your wife's embrace. Perhaps it's the allure of an unbreastfed bosom, the curvature of hips, the contour of lips, the shade of complexion, or even the timbre of a voice. If you indulge in the pursuit of every ephemeral craving, you shall remain forever unsatiated, for every woman boasts her own allure. It's akin to entering a banquet replete with an array of delicacies and attempting to savor them all, only to end up with a stomachache. No measure of wine is ever enough when one seeks to sample the entire spectrum; true satisfaction lies in savoring one's chosen vintage and relishing it eternally. Thus, the decision to uphold fidelity rests upon you, in honor of the woman who holds your heart. It's your prerogative to treat a singular woman like royalty, for a kingdom with multiple queens is destined for schism, its foundations eroding. Loving multitudes pales in comparison to loving a single soul in myriad ways, rendering you truly magnificent.

The sanctuary of fidelity holds boundless joy, as loving one woman above all others begets unparalleled fulfillment. A rolling stone gathers no moss, and a man who endlessly roams from one paramour to another shall never unearth genuine contentment in the tapestry of existence...

Who Qualifies as a Prudent Spouse?

A prudent spouse harbors a reverence for and devotion to the divine. Love and adoration flow effortlessly to the spouse and progeny. Nurturing is second nature, driven by visions and ambitions, upheld through tenacity and industry. Such a partner extends respect, support, and encouragement, embodying tolerance, empathy, flexibility, forgiveness, transparency, and reliability. A wise spouse crafts a domestic haven, not a purgatory, for loved ones.

Faithfulness defines a prudent spouse, an oath-keeper unswayed by temptation's seductive call. Cruelty finds no solace within these arms; instead, a regal demeanor graces both public appearances and intimate moments. Shields rise, defending the beloved against familial onslaughts or the throes of a daunting mother's ire. Solidarity reigns in times of trial—be it the quest for parenthood, health struggles, career setbacks, or periods of destitution—this partner stands steadfast. Detrimental companionships are eschewed, rendering company in harmony with virtue. Comfort and convenience are paramount, as burdens are shared, not borne alone.

Modesty defines the prudent spouse; humility persists despite accomplishments. Honor drives accountability, preferring resolution to escalation during disputes. A harbinger of peace, not strife, tranquillity reigns within the household, a testament to the wise spouse's demeanor. Marital leadership is embraced through exemplification, recognizing actions speak louder than words. Intimacy with the divine is nurtured, guiding familial aspirations skyward through prayer. The prudent spouse kindles the spouse's pride, an emblem of joyous matrimony.

I have been married for numerous years. Like any other man, I too face sexual temptations. However, I am resolute in my refusal to succumb to them. My wife is not only sufficient but surpasses any other temptation. To fully cherish and embrace a marriage with your spouse, you must find contentment in her companionship, including the intimate aspect. This is an unfiltered truth that many men struggle to accept. Let me be candid: no woman holds an inherent superiority over another. They possess similar qualities. The key difference between a faithful marriage and one marred by infidelity is contentment and a deep reverence for God. A man who truly reveres God would never claim an inability to settle for just one woman in marriage. Truth be told: men who go after other women, generally have LUST issues but they won't admit it. Men under the spirit of lust are never satisfied by one woman. Men controlled by this demon jump from women to women, using them and dumping them like used tissue! You are under the spirit of lust if you are easily aroused at the thought of the opposite sex and no matter how hard you try to control it, you end up sleeping with them! You are operating under this evil spirit if you must sleep with a woman whether married or single before you become normal. Lust has captured you if you are no longer sexually satisfied by your wife. Other people's wives or young single ladies are now your objects of interest. If you are easily turned on by the opposite sex and you secretly yearn for different sexual experience with them, you are possessed by the spirit of lust. Lust is simply desiring or pursuing what is not yours, no more, no less! Some people have a high sex drive that makes them easily respond to the opposite sex, that is understandable. As long as you control it and do not pursue the object of arousal, you do not have any problem. But if you must have sex with that person before you feel normal, you have a big problem at hand. Life is more than sex! You can't succeed in life by having sex with every Mary, Jane, and Susan! Your destiny is too precious to waste on the laps of strange women. Stop watching pornography pictures/videos. These actors are controlled by the spirit of lust, and it gets transferred to you. Pornography is a NO-NO if you must deal with this evil spirit tormenting you! Masturbation must be banned from your life if you want to live a sexually pure life. Solo sex doesn't satisfy. You will sooner or later look for a human being to do it with. Stop watching pornography. Stop moving with lusty men/women. Chronic fornicators/ adulterers should not be your friend, their spirit will get transferred to you. One single act of premarital sex will open you up for invasion of demons. Having sex with every woman you meet, doesn't prove that you are a man, it shows how empty you are on the inside.

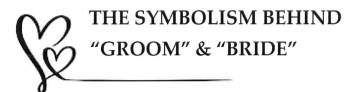

THE SYMBOLISM BEHIND "GROOM" & "BRIDE"

The appellations "Groom" and "Bride" bestowed upon partners on their wedding day encapsulate profound symbolism. "Groom" conveys the nurturing role of the husband-to-be, evoking images of preparation and care, much like the meticulous grooming of a prized steed before a grand event. It alludes to the husband's duty to safeguard and cherish his partner, mirroring the thoroughness required in tending to a cherished companion.

Conversely, "Bride" bespeaks purity and transformation, symbolizing the transition from a single existence to a shared journey of partnership. Like a flower that blooms in radiant splendor on its wedding day, the bride embodies the blossoming of love and unity, exuding an aura of beauty and grace. Just as a bride is adorned and cherished, so too is the journey of love adorned and held dear, as two lives intertwine in a harmonious union.

These titles reflect the profound roles each partner undertakes, unveiling a tapestry of commitment, care, and shared destiny woven together on the loom of marriage.

Consider this scenario: A man found himself growing weary of his wife within just six months of marriage. His discontentment was palpable, and he contemplated ending the relationship, convinced that he had made a grave error. But here's a perspective to ponder.

Numerous relationships have fractured because the envisioned image of a spouse didn't materialize. Yet, an essential aspect is often overlooked—the wedding day marks the inception of a transformative journey for the man. It is the moment when he is entrusted with the profound task of nurturing and guiding his bride toward becoming a wife. This is why he is aptly named the 'bridegroom' or 'groom.' The term "grooming" encompasses the patient nurturing, instructing, tending, and aiding someone's evolution into their destined role.

Therefore, it's postulated that the man who leads a woman to the marriage altar is mature enough to diligently groom her into the role of a wife. The transformation is not automatic; it necessitates the committed effort of the groom. To merely anticipate the bride's spontaneous transition into a wife disregards the essential process of grooming.

In retrospect, many of us, as men, harbor lofty and often impractical expectations as we enter into marriage. We yearn for a miraculous transformation in our partners, aspiring for them to align precisely with our envisioned ideal. Yet, we fail to recognize that our partners are not privy to our unspoken desires unless communicated.

Unrealistic expectations stem from an oversight—the failure to acknowledge that genuine change takes time and is feasible only when the individual in question comprehends the intended transformation. Therefore, before contemplating a parting of ways, it is imperative to reflect: Have you engaged in the process of grooming? Have you allowed time for mutual understanding? Remember, a turtle cannot become a hawk, and expecting such a transformation is counterproductive.

Divine providence often brings together individuals who complement each other through their unique strengths and weaknesses. Your spouse's strengths may lie where you falter, providing essential support where it is most needed. The predicament arises when we seek to instigate change before embracing acceptance. It's crucial to recognize that our partners hail from distinct backgrounds, necessitating a period of adaptation.

Rather than attempting to reshape her, extend acceptance, love, and guidance. Exercise patience, for this is the essence of grooming.

While she is destined to be your wife, she is your bride for now—a period during which you are entrusted with the task of grooming her. Refrain from voicing complaints; instead, understand that she is a turtle while you are a hawk. Be patient as she takes her time to flourish.

The conviction that your marriage is beyond redemption is unfounded. Embrace patience and allow divine intervention to guide your path.

SEX IS SWEET

Most downfalls of men are caused by MULTIPLE girlfriends. Sex is a spiritual encounter I stand to be corrected not every girl has a good spirit, some are demon, some has poison in between their legs, some are killers and destiny destroyers, be careful A man who can control his sexual urge is a man who can live many years on earth. Having many girlfriends does not make you a man. It only makes you a womanizer a cheat and a boy. A real man has only one woman in his life. For the fact that you are good in bed does not make you a man. A real man is the man who does not run away from his responsibility but faces it squarely. You don't need to sag your trousers and walk round the street before girls will love you. In fact, it is only small boys that sag trousers, and it is premature little girls that fall in love with men who sag trousers. Don't use and dump ladies. Remember the law of karma. Whatever you do you will receive the reward. If you cannot make her your wife, don't make her a mother. If she can't be your wife don't sleep with her. Do not always obey your erection. Most times our erections mislead us in the wrong direction. Control your erection. Don't let your erection control you. If you don't control your erection, you will have few days on earth with much poverty. You may insult me, but it doesn't matter to me now, because am done telling you this. It is not everything you see under skirt that you should hustle to get; some skirts contain snakes that will bite you and leave you uncomfortable. Control your sex urge, Self-control and abstinence in most cases pays a lot. Do not date a lady because she has sexy curves, nice boobs and shapes Those things are just packaging and packaging can be very deceptive avoid, such. Respect any lady that loves you. Yes, it's not easy for a lady to throw her love on you and support your future. Do not beat any woman, even if she is not your wife. Real man learns how to keep secret. BE THE REAL MAN.

Many men will say each time she goes by I get an erection. There is nothing wrong in getting an erection so don't get wrong. In fact, let's talk about that thing call Erection. Erection represents a state of heightened sexual desire in a man, occurring as a preparatory phase for potential sexual activity. While experiencing an erection is a natural occurrence, responding to its impulses remains a matter of personal choice. Every instance of an erection carries with it a corresponding responsibility. Men of wisdom exercise command over their erections, whereas those who heedlessly submit to their desires are displaying folly.

An unregulated erection possesses the potential to lead an individual down a perilous path. Unsolicited erections do not discriminate based on factors such as an individual's sanctity, righteousness, vigor, or age. Only through self-control and self-discipline can one effectively manage and restrain the urges associated with an erection.

Numerous individuals have failed to assume their role as responsible fathers due to an inability to govern their erections. Certain individuals find themselves incarcerated because of yielding to the dictates of their ill-advised erections. Opportunities of significant magnitude have slipped through the grasp of many, all because their erections compelled them. Some are confined to their beds, prisoners of their uncontrollable erections.

The irrationality of an erection often lies in its indiscriminate nature. Unchecked, an erection has led even the most illustrious monarchs to the beds of their subordinates, an act of foolishness. This heedless desire has coerced individuals into intimate relationships with their own siblings and led fathers to transgress against their daughters. Even those who have embraced a role of spiritual guidance have fallen prey to the allure of their unbridled erections, causing them to stray from their intended paths. Truly, the consequences of this unthinking erection are profound.

The measure of a strong man is not solely determined by his physical prowess or his territorial conquests; rather, it hinges upon his mastery over his own bodily urges. History does not lack for powerful figures, yet Samson's story illustrates how an erection can render even the mightiest weak, as he succumbed to the embrace of a woman. David's triumphs over giants and nations were overshadowed by his inability to conquer his own desires, as exemplified by his vulnerability in the presence of Bathsheba, a woman married to one of his loyal subjects. The unchecked erection led Reuben astray, sealing his fate and the destinies of those who followed him.

Avoid allowing your erection to undermine your life's purpose!

An erection serves as a testament to your masculinity yet permitting it to dictate your actions in every sphere showcases a fundamental weakness.

A man who cannot govern his own erection is ill-equipped to steer the course of his life.

Your erection's potential for misguidance is diminished when channeled solely within the bounds of marriage.

Refuse to be led by your erection; instead, follow the path of your aspirations.

You might possess the wisdom of Solomon, the praise of David, or the faith of Abraham, but if you lack the discipline of Joseph, your fate could mirror the destruction that befell Samson. Reflect upon this sobering notion.

A TRIUMPH OF SELF-CONTROL

Erections are a natural manifestation of male desire, a precursor to the pursuit of intimacy. Yet, the true measure of a man lies not in the erection itself, but in the control, he wields over his impulses. An erection, uncontrolled, can lead to grievous consequences. Self-discipline is the guiding force that reigns in these desires, preventing them from dictating one's actions.

It's a choice: to obey the whims of an erection or to assert dominion over it. Responsibility accompanies each erection, as its influence can be both profound and perilous. The wise harness its power, while the foolish allow themselves to be ensnared. History bears witness to mighty men whose unchecked erections led them astray, derailing their destinies.

Samson, the epitome of strength, succumbed to the allure of desire, yielding his power to Delilah's seductive charms. Even a man of David's stature, who vanquished giants and conquered kingdoms, faltered in the face of lust, succumbing to Bathsheba's allure. Erection can be the crucible of greatness or the harbinger of downfall, depending on the mastery we exert.

Self-control transcends physical prowess; it encompasses the mind, spirit, and soul. It stands as the guardian of destiny, a testament to a man's mastery over himself. Embrace self-control as your compass, navigating you away from treacherous waters toward a life of fulfillment and purpose.

Marriage is a commitment to one woman. The reality is that men who pursue other women often struggle with feelings of intense desire, though they may not openly acknowledge it. Those who are consumed by lust often find it difficult to be content with a single partner. Such individuals, driven by this overpowering urge, move from one person to another, treating them as disposable objects.

The grip of lust becomes apparent when one becomes easily aroused by the opposite sex and finds it challenging to control these impulses, eventually succumbing to sexual encounters. This detrimental influence manifests when the need to engage in physical intimacy, whether with a married or single woman, becomes a requirement to feel normal.

Lust takes hold when the satisfaction from one's spouse diminishes, leading to an unhealthy fascination with other women, whether they are married or single. The yearning for novel and diverse sexual experiences signifies the presence of this insidious spirit. Lust is, in essence, the pursuit of what is forbidden or unattainable.

While a heightened libido is natural for some, it remains manageable as long as it is controlled and not acted upon. However, if the urge to engage in sexual activity with someone else becomes a necessity for emotional balance, a serious issue arises.

Life encompasses far more than mere physical pleasure. Achieving success and fulfillment requires steering clear of promiscuity and valuing one's destiny too greatly to squander it on fleeting liaisons.

Abstain from viewing explicit content, as it perpetuates the influence of lust, passed on from the performers. Reject pornography, and avoid associating with those who exhibit lustful behavior, as their inclinations can affect you.

Masturbation should be eliminated from your life if you seek a sexually pure existence. Solitary gratification is ultimately unsatisfying and may lead to a quest for human connection.

Avoiding pornography, refraining from mingling with lustful individuals, and distancing yourself from chronic promiscuity or adultery is crucial, as their negative energies can permeate your own.

Engaging in premarital sex opens one up to spiritual vulnerability. The pursuit of countless partners is not a testament to masculinity; rather, it reflects inner emptiness.

Recognize that while sexual intimacy can be pleasurable, it is often multiple relationships that cause the downfall of men.

Sexual encounters possess a spiritual aspect. It's important to discern the nature of those you engage with, as not every person carries a positive energy. Some may harbor negative intentions or harmful influences.

The ability to control one's sexual urges demonstrates true strength and longevity. A man's character is not defined by numerous relationships but by his commitment and integrity. A genuine man maintains loyalty to one woman, facing responsibilities head-on.

External appearances, such as sagging trousers, do not define your worth or attract genuine affection. Immature actions do not foster genuine connections.

Treating women with respect and honoring their feelings is crucial. Appreciate the significance of someone's love and support for your future.

Physical force should never be used against a woman, even if she isn't your spouse. True masculinity involves discretion and empathy.

Real men understand the value of confidentiality and trustworthiness.

Ultimately, strive to be an authentic man of integrity and self-control.

However, one might argue that other women continually attempt to entice me with their bodies.

Certain men lament their perpetual struggles with lust, attributing it to the relentless exposure of women flaunting their seductive physiques directly in front of them. No matter how earnestly they strive to avert their gaze, the allure proves insurmountable. My dear friend, you must address the inclinations of your eyes and desires, lest you descend into a state of psychological disarray.

There exist women who remain resolute, undeterred by admonitions as they provocatively sway their hips, unabashedly displaying their posterior assets regardless of vocal protests. Prostitutes continue to parade in scanty attire, while sex workers brazenly accentuate their cleavage, and even inexperienced young girls, mature women, and married ladies may inadvertently tantalize. The timelier you cultivate self-restraint and relinquish excuses for indulging in lustful desires, the more advantageous it shall be.

I heard a story where a fair-skinned married woman sought her counsel following childbirth. She bemoaned how nursing had caused soreness in her nipples. In an impulsive gesture, she exposed her ample, taut breast in front of the counselor's spouse, while pointing out the afflicted nipple. The counselor was taken aback, nearly imploring the woman to conceal her provocative display. The husband of the counselor remained composed and attentive, unwavering despite the situation — a testament to his maturity.

Your emotional fortitude warrants refinement; learn to stand firm in the face of provocations. Consider the hypothetical scenario of becoming a medical practitioner — would you then engage in trysts with every patient?

Indeed, men are often swayed by visual stimuli, and women should exercise prudence in their attire choices. If you profess to be a devout, spirit-filled child of God, yet parade about in provocatively minuscule garments and subsequently fall victim to a heinous act, your grievances may receive a less sympathetic response. It is imperative to acknowledge the correlation between attire and perception.

Nevertheless, this should not furnish men with an excuse to traverse society with conspicuous arousal. You are a man, not a child. A true man exerts mastery over his impulses, consistently monitoring his surroundings to shield his gaze from depravity. Command your eyes and the movement of your head. Steer your legs toward righteous paths and direct your hands to remain inert when propriety demands. May you forever evade the pitfalls set by malevolent forces.

THE BEAUTY OF INTIMACY

I find profound joy in sharing intimate moments with my wife, as the connection goes beyond mere physicality. Engaging in lovemaking is a passionate experience that ignites our senses. It's a dance of emotions and desires, encompassing every inch of our beings, from head to toe. The crescendo of sensation that courses through our bodies at its zenith is truly electric! I jestingly pray that my wife's overwhelming sensuality won't one day lead to my untimely demise!

True intimacy is an art, requiring substantial effort and commitment. It's a far cry from casual encounters, demanding a considerable investment of time and energy. Such encounters don't begin with a hasty leap into the bed; that approach would never cultivate genuine satisfaction. Authentic sexual union, resulting in earth-shattering climaxes for both partners, originates in the realm of mental connection. Until my wife and I delve into the intimate realm of each other's minds, we cannot fully relish the physical aspect.

Understanding, communication, and empathy form the foundation of this mental connection. I recognize that no woman is frigid within the confines of the bedroom. If Jesus had a spouse, she would undoubtedly radiate unparalleled passion and desire. His ability to make a woman feel cherished and valued would be unparalleled, akin to Mary Magdalene's adoration, symbolized by her anointing his feet with expensive perfumed oil. Every woman is a vibrant force of sensuality, transcending societal norms and religious roles.

Once we embark on the journey of understanding her inner world—her thoughts, feelings, strengths, and vulnerabilities—she transforms into a supernova of passion, a sexual dynamo unparalleled by any before her. It lies within my power to shape her erotic persona, a responsibility I hold with utmost reverence. Should love-making lack its magic, the fault ultimately rests with me, for I am the conductor of our passionate symphony.

"The husband should fulfill his marital duty to his wife, and likewise the wife to her husband. The wife's body does not belong to her alone but also to her husband. In the same way, the husband's body does not belong to him alone but also to his wife. Do not deprive each other except by mutual consent and for a time" (1 Corinthians 7:3-5a).

Marriage holds multifaceted practical functions, yet its paramount essence lies in mirroring the divine bond between Christ and His Church, often referred to as His Bride. Within this sacred union, we find resonant echoes of sweet joy, profound intimacy, and unwavering commitment. These qualities, so beautifully intertwined, unveil to me the depth of the Lord's desires for His cherished Bride, as well as the abundant blessings He yearns to lavish upon her.

Let us embark on an alternative exploration of the realm of intimacy and sexuality within marriage. Instead of delving into the pragmatic necessities, marital obligations, or the strategies to attain them, I invite us to contemplate the sanctity, allure, tenderness, and privilege inherent in the intimate connection shared with our husbands. Let's cast an unreserved gaze upon the act of physical intimacy and the realm of closeness, perceiving them through the lens of our Savior. In this perspective, we shall endeavor to transcend the misconceptions of impurity, the utilitarian view of procreation, and the notion of another task to fulfill as a "virtuous spouse." Instead, our aim is to perceive these aspects as the exquisite imagery they were originally designed to embody. We shall draw parallels between the intimacy with our earthly partners and the spiritual communion with our divine Creator.

In the ancient words of Genesis 2:24, we read, "Therefore a man shall leave his father and mother and be joined to his wife, and they shall become one flesh." In an earlier verse, Genesis 1:28, the divine injunction to "be fruitful and multiply" resonates. Verse 31 reinforces that "God saw everything that He had made, and indeed it was very good." It is crucial to recognize that sex was an intentional creation of God. He established marriage as the sole sanctuary for intimacy, reserving it for the covenant between husband and wife. He not only initiated this sacred union but also beheld it as a profoundly virtuous creation. As Martha Peace eloquently elucidates in her book "The Excellent Wife," the conjugal bond serves as a divine gift, fostering both physical connection and the potential for life. This act, which God has pronounced "very good," stands as a testimony to the world's distortion and corruption, rather than reflecting its innate sanctity.

Sex and intimacy within the marital context are channels of delight and fulfillment. God endowed men and women with innate desires that He intended to be gratified within the framework of marriage. It is a misconception to regard sex as impure or immoral; when embraced within God's ordained boundaries, it transforms into a sacred and holy expression of love. The fervent verses of Proverbs 5:18-19 exhort us to celebrate the delight and captivation found within the bond of marriage.

The poetic narrative of the Song of Solomon recounts the poignant journey of a husband and wife, tracing their love story from the fervent throes of courtship to the serene beauty of their later years. This lyrical masterpiece has been interpreted both allegorically, symbolizing God's love for His people, and literally, depicting the profound love between spouses. In my perspective, it embodies both interpretations. The intimacy and love shared between a husband and wife find parallels in the relationship believers share with their Creator. Though the expressions of intimacy differ, the depth of connection remains congruent.

Let us now turn our gaze to select passages from the Song of Solomon, inviting a dual perspective as we savor the passion and elation between husbands and wives while simultaneously glimpsing the ardor and longing within the divine relationship. The opening lines, "Let him kiss me with the kisses of his mouth—For your love is better than wine," set a tone of fervent yearning, an emotion that stems not from a place of impurity but rather from the purity of love within God's design.

In chapter 2, verses 16-17, we encounter an exultation of mutual ownership and fervor, echoed in the subsequent verses of chapter 7, which sing praises to the beloved's beauty and desire. These verses mirror the spiritual intensity that believers experience in their relationship with the Lord.

# ENHANCING INTIMACY IN MARRIAGE

Now, as we turn our attention to practical considerations, let us explore how husbands can nurture excellence in intimacy within their marriages:

Grasp the Purpose

Recognize that intimacy is divinely orchestrated, bearing multiple purposes. It serves in procreation, a shared role in the miracle of creation. Embrace this privilege of partnering with God to bring forth life.

Pleasure

Revel in the God-given delight of sexual intimacy. Understand that sex is not a sinful act when engaged within marriage; it is a beautiful, holy, and pleasurable gift.

Imagery

Comprehend the symbolic resonance between marital intimacy and the longing for oneness with God. Just as God's desire for unity with His Bride is portrayed through imagery, so too does marital intimacy embody this divine concept.

Beyond the Act

Expand your perspective beyond sexual intercourse. Cherish the gentle touches, the moments of shared affection, and the act of simply being close. These are vital to sustaining a healthy marriage.

Mutual Fulfillment

Delve into your spouse's needs and desires. Recognize the parallel between emotional and physical intimacy and take active steps to meet those needs.

Creativity

Engage in open communication with your spouse to explore new avenues of connection and pleasure. Draw inspiration from the passionate verses of the Song of Solomon to invigorate your marital intimacy.

Enduring Love

Acknowledge that the intensity of passion may ebb and flow, yet the commitment to nurture intimacy remains constant. Embrace the ebb and flow, ensuring that the flame of intimacy remains alive.

Let us celebrate the precious gift of intimacy within marriage, upholding its sanctity and cherishing its manifold purposes. Just as we joyfully anticipate the heavenly embrace of our Savior, let us treasure the earthly union with our beloved spouses, embracing the profound depth of love that binds us together. By abiding in love, we manifest the divine purpose of intimate connection, drawing parallels between our earthly bonds and our eternal relationship with the Creator. As we bask in the words of the Beloved, may we resoundingly proclaim, "I sit in his shade with great delight, and his (her) fruit is sweet to my taste. He brought me to the banqueting house, and his banner over me was love." (Song of Solomon 2:3b-4)

How can couples foster intimacy within their marriage? Marriage is meant to be the most profound and intimate connection a person can experience. It should surpass the intimacy found in friendships, parent-child relationships, and romantic partnerships. However, it's unfortunate that many couples find themselves feeling distant and isolated within their marriage.

Given that humans consist of body, soul, and spirit (as mentioned in 1 Thessalonians 5:23 and Hebrews 4:12), couples need to nurture all these dimensions to cultivate intimacy. This includes nurturing their emotional connection (soul), physical intimacy (body), and spiritual bond (spirit) within the marriage. All three aspects are essential, and neglecting any one of them can lead to a lack of the desired intimacy.

DEVELOPING EMOTIONAL INTIMACY

When it comes to fostering emotional intimacy, one can draw inspiration from the relationship between Christ and the church. In John 15:15, Jesus refers to his followers as friends rather than servants, highlighting the depth of connection he shares with them. This friendship is characterized by openness and sharing, as Jesus revealed divine truths to his followers.

Similarly, married couples can strengthen their emotional intimacy by regularly sharing their lives, thoughts, fears, and concerns with one another. This practice of open communication helps build a strong bond of friendship and, consequently, intimacy. Despite the busyness of life, making intentional time for such communication is crucial. Evenings, when work and other obligations are done, often provide an ideal opportunity for couples to connect on a deeper level.

Practical Steps to Foster Emotional Intimacy

Below are some practical steps to enhance emotional intimacy:

- Set aside dedicated time each day for open and heartfelt sharing.

- As life gets busier, prioritize intimate conversations in the evenings.

- Recognize and address distractions or activities that hinder emotional connection.

- Preserve intimacy amidst distractions. In a world filled with distractions, it's important to safeguard intimacy from potential intrusions. Just as with our relationship with God, where we sometimes prioritize lesser matters over our spiritual connection, couples should be vigilant about protecting their emotional intimacy. Just like the story of Mary and Martha, who had different priorities when Jesus visited, couples should avoid getting caught up in tasks that pull them away from each other.

- Balance priorities. Managing a home, raising children, and handling other responsibilities can be demanding, especially as a family grows. However, maintaining emotional intimacy remains a crucial aspect of a healthy marriage. Some couples adopt strategies, like setting a designated time after which they focus solely on each other. This prioritization not only strengthens the bond between partners but also serves as a valuable lesson for children, emphasizing the importance of the marital relationship.

Cultivating intimacy requires dedication and awareness. By prioritizing emotional connection, couples can navigate the challenges of modern life while nurturing a profound and fulfilling marital relationship.

Authentic closeness, though frequently diverted from, can often be hindered by various distractions. Activities such as watching television, browsing the internet, playing video games, or being on the phone can serve as ways to avoid or sidestep intimacy.

One suggestion: refraining from turning on the TV during the initial year of marriage. This foundational period sets the tone for the rest of the marriage. Just as in the Old Testament, where a newlywed soldier was required to remain home and bring joy to his wife for the first year of marriage (Deut 24:5), the early stages of marriage establish both healthy and unhealthy patterns. If a couple establishes habits centered on watching and doing rather than being and sharing, it could lead to detrimental consequences later in the marriage. It is not uncommon for couples to realize after years of marriage that they never truly knew each other. This could result from establishing unhealthy patterns early on, where intimacy blockers kept them from genuinely understanding one another.

This insight is particularly relevant to marriage, especially during the pivotal first year that forms the bedrock for the relationship's longevity. Do you desire a marriage where your partner comes home, gives you a quick kiss, and then immerses themselves in the internet, TV, or phone for hours before bedtime? Being cautious of these tendencies that can potentially harm relationships is important. Safeguard against intimacy inhibitors and allocate daily time for genuine sharing, active listening, and being together.

NURTURING FRIENDSHIP

Having said all that, a sense of balance is vital in marriage. Couples should engage in moments of open sharing and attentive listening, but they should also partake in shared activities like reading, exercising, watching movies, traveling, and more. Regrettably, many couples enter marriage believing they share numerous enjoyable activities, only to discover their disparate interests after the first year. During courtship, a woman might tolerate watching sports with her boyfriend just to be with him, but once married, she may opt out of watching Sunday football in favor of her own pursuits. Similarly, a man could accompany his girlfriend to the mall during courtship, but in marriage, he may choose to stay home instead of joining her on a Saturday shopping trip. The early fervor of passion often blurs the perception of one's future spouse, and couples should remain cognizant of this potential discrepancy.

Whether this scenario materializes or not, it is crucial for couples to identify activities they can enjoy together to foster and enhance intimacy. Christ was constantly present with His followers, the disciples, sharing every experience with them (cf. Matt 17:1, John 15:15). To safeguard and nurture our marriages, it is prudent to contemplate and schedule joint activities, setting aside weekly or monthly dates to engage in these shared pursuits. "The plans of the diligent lead to profit as surely as haste leads to poverty" (Proverbs 21:5).

Of course, it's natural for spouses to have differing preferences when it comes to activities. However, out of love for each other, they should occasionally participate in their partner's interests. The wife might occasionally watch a football game, while the husband could occasionally join in watching a romantic comedy. Serving our spouse out of love, even by engaging in their preferred activities, strengthens the bond of friendship.

Cultivating Friendship through Weekly Date Nights. Furthermore, a wise practice for couples is to establish a dedicated weekly date night. Choose a convenient evening to go out and engage in something special. Guard this time from the demands of daily life, and when unforeseen circumstances arise, make it a priority to reschedule. The cost of the date night is not as important as the quality time spent together without interruptions.

One of the enduring truths of marriage is that understanding your spouse deeply will take a lifetime, as they continually grow and evolve. Therefore, it is essential to approach friendship-building within marriage as a deliberate discipline, investing effort to cultivate intimacy.

Physical Intimacy

Moving on, couples must also work on fostering intimacy through physical connection. God intended sexual intimacy to serve as a potent catalyst for deepening the bond in marriage. Often referred to as the "litmus test" of a marriage, sex can reveal the degree of closeness between partners and contribute to its expansion.

If a married couple finds themselves going through extended periods without engaging in sexual activity, it might be an appropriate juncture to assess the state of their relationship. Questions like, "Is our partnership still strong?" and "Am I meeting my spouse's needs?" could come to mind.

When reflecting on the role of sexual intimacy, it's also pertinent to consider the strategies that negative influences may employ within the realm of marriage. Prior to marriage, these influences may focus on tempting couples toward premarital sex. However, within marriage, the focus shifts towards tempting couples to abstain from sexual relations. This dynamic might seem contradictory, especially for young married couples who previously struggled to contain their passion before marriage. Yet, in the context of marriage, sexual intimacy can sometimes become less vibrant and more routine. This shift is a point where negative influences, like a metaphorical representation of Satan, might seek to diminish a couple's closeness by reducing their sexual connection. Further exploration of this concept will follow in subsequent discussions.

For now, let's delve into the intended purposes of sex as outlined by a spiritual perspective:

One of God's fundamental purposes for sex is to foster unity and intimacy within a marital relationship. In Genesis 2:24, it is stated, "Therefore a man shall leave his father and mother and be joined to his wife, and they shall become one flesh." This notion of becoming "one flesh" directly alludes to sexual union. This concept is further reinforced by 1 Corinthians

6:16, which describes how a man who engages in sexual relations with a harlot becomes "one flesh" with her. The act of sexual intimacy symbolizes the unity and intimacy that a married couple cultivates. Interestingly, this symbolism is extended to represent God's intimacy and covenant with the nation of Israel, as seen in Ezekiel 16:8.

Another purpose of sex, in alignment with God's plan, is procreation. This intention is evident in the directive provided in Genesis 1:27-28, where God blesses humanity and instructs them to be fruitful and multiply. This desire for godly offspring is also emphasized in Malachi 2:15, where the unity of husband and wife is portrayed to generate godly descendants.

Pleasure and enjoyment within the context of marriage are also highlighted as purposes of sex. Scriptures such as Proverbs 5:18-19 and Song of Songs 7:6-12 depict the beauty and delight of sexual intimacy between spouses. This enjoyment is celebrated as an expression of love and pleasure shared between partners.

Serving one's spouse is another essential purpose of sexual intimacy, as emphasized in 1 Corinthians 7:3-4. The mutual responsibility to fulfill each other's needs is underscored, reinforcing the idea that each partner's body belongs to the other. There is an acknowledgment that temporary periods of abstaining from sexual activity can be agreed upon for focused devotion or other valid reasons.

SIGNIFICANCE OF SEXUAL INTIMACY

Sexual intimacy holds significant meaning and purpose within a marital relationship. It serves as a conduit for unity, intimacy, procreation, enjoyment, and the mutual care of spouses. Understanding these purposes can help guide married couples in nurturing a healthy and fulfilling sexual connection. Here are some ways you can discover purpose in sexual intimacy:

Pray

Reunite in prayer, preventing Satan from exploiting your lack of self-control.

Explore Paul's Teaching on Marital Intimacy

Paul instructed that within marriage, both the wife and husband should willingly share ownership of their bodies (v. 4). The use of physical intimacy as a tool for manipulation or punishment is discouraged. Paul emphasized the importance of not withholding physical affection from one another, except by mutual agreement for spiritual purposes (v. 5).

Seek Guidance on Sexual Relations

Upon entering marriage, couples should make a commitment to offer themselves to each other even when upset or not initially inclined. This approach aligns with scriptural teachings, and the act of saying, "Though I may not currently feel inclined, I am willing to serve you in this way," underscores the concept of viewing sexual intimacy as a means of ministering to one another. Married couples should consider sex as a way to fulfill each other's needs rather than indulging their own desires.

Knowing The True Purpose of Marital Sex

Unfortunately, marital sex sometimes centers around self-gratification rather than service. This misalignment with God's intentions can lead to feelings of being used or unsatisfied by a partner. However, this deviates from God's plan. Philippians 2:3-4 encourages selflessness and considering others' needs. In the realm of sexual intimacy, the husband should prioritize the wife's pleasure, and vice versa.

Knowing Differing Libidos

In many marriages, one partner may have a stronger sexual desire than the other. As God's design calls for prioritizing the other's pleasure, this could result in one partner engaging in sex more frequently than desired, while the other may have less frequent encounters. Striving to serve each other's interests in the sexual aspect of the relationship remains crucial.

Prayer and Grace

If a spouse lacks the desire to serve their partner sexually, prayer for grace is advisable. Continuously seeking ways to better serve one another within the sexual relationship honors God's design for marriage. The understanding of available grace further supports this practice.

Ministering through Grace

Couples should approach sexual intimacy with the awareness that divine grace is present (James 4:6, Galatians 5:22-23, John 15:5). God intends to provide grace to foster love, service, and blessing within the sexual union. Regularly seeking divine anointing for their union is recommended.

Guard Against Temptation

The Purpose of Sex: First Corinthians 7:1-2 emphasizes that marriage and sexual relations within it are meant to shield couples from the allure of sexual immorality. Paul's instruction underscores the significance of consistent sexual intimacy in marriage. A lack of consistency can open the door to various temptations, such as lust, pornography, adultery, feelings of unloved or undesired, and emotional turmoil.

Cultivate Marital Protection

When sexual consistency is absent, it exposes couples to Satan's enticements. For instance, wives may experience feelings of unattractiveness and neglect, especially after childbirth. Inconsistent sexual intimacy can also render husbands more susceptible to sexual temptation, particularly in professional settings. Recognizing sexual intimacy as a protective barrier against the enemy's schemes is a prudent perspective.

Maintain Spiritual Discipline

An illustrative example is a friend who encountered challenges in the bedroom shortly after marriage. Satan exploited this vulnerability, causing insecurities and discord. To counter such attacks, couples should commit to marital fidelity in this aspect, not merely as a means of enhancing their relationship, but as a strategy for safeguarding it. Some churches have initiated marriage campaigns in recent years, where couples engage in a spiritual discipline of daily sexual intimacy for a designated period. This practice serves to fortify the marital bond and protect it from external pressures.

Enhance Marital Well-being

While it might seem like an ambitious endeavor, the underlying principle is deeply rooted in biblical wisdom. Establishing a robust strategy to foster marital health is a prudent approach. Couples are encouraged to consider implementing a weekly plan for nurturing their sexual intimacy. It is essential to acknowledge that various distractions, such as busyness, exhaustion, parenting, and other commitments, can hinder couples from experiencing the blessings of a fulfilling sexual relationship. Proverbs 21:5 highlights the significance of diligent planning, affirming that thoughtful preparation leads to prosperity, whereas haste can result in detriment. This principle underscores the importance of intentional actions to ensure success and fulfillment.

However, a word of caution is pertinent, especially concerning the phase of parenthood. The arrival of children introduces new dynamics that can impact marital intimacy. While the blessings of parenthood are undeniable, they can also open avenues for challenges to arise in the realm of sexual intimacy. Often, children become the focal point of a marriage, and in certain cultural contexts, practices such as prolonged co-sleeping with children can further complicate matters. In these scenarios, couples must adopt strategic approaches to safeguard and strengthen their bond. It's crucial to recognize that challenges to marital harmony persist even in the presence of children, and vigilance is required to thwart any disruptions. Consequently, Christian couples are urged to exercise wisdom and prudence in safeguarding their union.

With this perspective in mind, here are some strategies to enrich the sexual dimension of marriage:

- Engage in open and honest communication about sexual intimacy.

- Plan regular date nights to nurture emotional and physical connection.

- Infuse flirtatious gestures throughout the day to maintain a sense of excitement.

- Incorporate prayer into your journey of intimacy.

- Embrace creativity in your intimate moments.

- Thoughtfully explore Christian literature that offers valuable insights without compromising reverence. A particularly noteworthy insight from Christian literature is the recognition of the unique physiological and emotional differences between men and women. This understanding underscores the significance of a husband's attentive and considerate approach, extending beyond the bedroom. Serving and connecting with one another through touch, communication, and acts of love contribute to a deeper bond and mutual satisfaction.

In summation, the act of sexual intimacy is a divine celebration designed to enrich the marital bond. It serves as a platform for cultivating unity, fostering intimacy, and experiencing pure joy. Nevertheless, it is a realm susceptible to external attacks, and couples must proactively safeguard and nurture it.

NURTURING SPIRITUAL INTIMACY

Regrettably, the spiritual dimension of intimacy often goes overlooked within marriages, despite its immense potential to enhance connection. Just as individuals dedicate efforts to nourish their minds and bodies, the spirit requires attention. This spiritual aspect is often the missing link in achieving a thriving and successful marriage.

Distinguishing humanity from mere animals, the presence of a spiritual connection with God elevates mankind. Neglecting this aspect can lead to a sense of incompleteness, akin to the instincts that drive animals. Throughout the Genesis narrative, the close communion between man and God is evident, emphasizing the innate need for a relationship with the Divine.

To foster spiritual intimacy, couples are encouraged to consider the following practices:

Dedicate regular moments for communal prayer and engaging with God's Word as a family.

Actively participate in worship and fellowship within a Bible-centered church.

Embrace opportunities for joint service to God and others, such as hospitality and community outreach.

Cultivating spiritual intimacy enriches the marital bond, reinforcing the idea of becoming "one flesh" through shared spiritual growth

(Genesis 2:24). By weaving together individual devotions, collective worship, and joint acts of service, couples forge a deeper connection and experience a more fulfilling partnership.

In essence, intimacy within a marriage encompasses multiple dimensions—friendship, sexuality, and spirituality—each requiring deliberate cultivation. Drawing from biblical wisdom, couples can formulate a comprehensive plan to enhance these facets of intimacy. This approach ensures that the marital union flourishes, guided by open communication, shared experiences, and a profound connection with God. By prioritizing these aspects, couples are poised to embark on a journey of lasting love, unity, and fulfillment.

BALANCING DESIRE AND DEVOTION

Dear gentlemen, let it be known that women, too, harbor their own sexual desires. Dismissing their inclinations as solely a male trait is a fallacy. Both genders share a common yearning. While fidelity, respect for vows, and the fear of divine consequences often keep women's impulses in check, they are not immune to temptation. Respect and honor your wives' self-discipline; their fortitude should never be taken for granted. Remember, adultery is a transgression regardless of the perpetrator.

Cherish your wives wholeheartedly, treating them with the reverence they deserve. Lavish them with tokens of affection, be it in the form of fragrant perfumes, elegant attire, or attentive gestures. Such care kindles a fire of ardor that often deters the allure of infidelity. Elevate your wife to a queenly status, a luminary in your life, and the seductive mirage of side liaisons will lose its allure.

Participate in domestic responsibilities, share the load when fatigue sets in, and extend a helping hand in times of need. Engaging in the routine tasks of daily life fortifies your connection, transforming it into an unbreakable bond. Demonstrate love through actions, not just words. Such gestures forge an unbreakable alliance that shields your marital realm from external temptations fostering mutual respect.

What is Mutual Respect?

Mutual respect embodies a straightforward principle: treating your spouse or partner with consideration and courtesy. It involves avoiding behaviors that exhibit rudeness or disrespect, such as refraining from name-calling, insults, and belittlement. Moreover, it encompasses refraining from adopting a sarcastic tone, ignoring, or sidestepping your partner. At its core, mutual respect entails valuing your partner's opinions, desires, and principles, regarding them as deserving of genuine attention.

Though the concept is uncomplicated, consistently upholding respectful treatment in a relationship demands a dedicated endeavor. Respect surpasses mere avoidance of negative conduct; it thrives on the presence of affirmative actions. In practice, demonstrating respect toward your spouse or partner involves actions like considering their viewpoints, involving them in decisions that impact them, displaying a proactive interest in their daily life (including work and interests), and engaging in compromise and negotiation regarding significant matters that affect both of you and your family.

While this compilation of behaviors is by no means exhaustive, it captures the fundamental essence of fostering a marriage or relationship built on mutual respect.

Recognizing Signs of Mutual Respect

In intimate relationships, the significance of mutual respect has been extensively examined and is deemed a pivotal element of any thriving partnership. However, detecting its presence isn't always straightforward. This exploration delves into the telltale signs of mutual respect, aiding you in gauging its existence within your relationship.

Primary indicators of mutual respect encompass active listening and forthright communication. When partners lend genuine attention without interruption or disregard, and engage in candid, truthful discussions, it showcases their mutual trust and respect. This willingness to share thoughts and emotions sans judgment underscores the depth of their respect.

Additionally, independence and parity exemplify mutual respect. This entails preserving individual identities, nurturing personal pursuits, and treating each other as equals. By supporting each other's personal evolution, joint decision-making, and equitable task-sharing, the manifestation of mutual respect is evident.

Furthermore, compromise and trust are pivotal constituents of mutual respect. Demonstrating willingness to compromise and trust each other underscores reverence for individual needs, choices, and actions. Recognizing these signs empowers you to ascertain their presence and work towards their augmentation.

MUTUAL RESPECT WITHIN MARRIAGE

In the realm of building robust and wholesome relationships, mutual respect occupies a central role. This involves displaying consideration and esteeming each other's viewpoints, sentiments, and boundaries, facilitating conflict resolution and joint growth. Presented here are ten instances illuminating mutual respect in a relationship:

Engaged Listening

Devoting time to genuinely comprehend each other's perspectives proves pivotal in a relationship. Partners who actively immerse themselves in each other's thoughts, emotions, and concerns convey a genuine valuation and respect, enriching overall communication and connection.

Candid Dialogue

Effective, unguarded communication remains indispensable for sustaining mutual respect. Transparency coupled with respectful discourse serves as an emblematic illustration of mutual esteem, nurturing a more robust bond.

Fostering Aspirations

True respect entails championing each other's ambitions, nurturing personal and professional pursuits. Encouraging and supporting these goals strengthens the relationship's vitality.

Honoring Personal Space

Acknowledging the need for solitude and individual space constitutes a cornerstone of mutual respect. By affording each other privacy and solitary moments, profound respect for well-being is manifested, enabling personal rejuvenation and pursuit of interests.

Shared Domestic Responsibilities

Collectively upholding domestic harmony underscores mutual respect. Shared responsibilities epitomize regard for each other's time and energy, engendering a harmonious coexistence.

Empathetic Sensitivity

Respect is further evident in empathetic responses to distress or agitation. Partners who empathize and comprehend each other's emotions convey profound care and respect for each other's feelings.

Sidestepping Critique:

Present times often witness blame and criticism, detrimental to relationships. Constructive conflict resolution, marked by compromise and shared solutions, signifies mutual respect, nurturing a harmonious environment.

Owning Up and Amending

Acknowledging errors and making amends is a potent demonstration of mutual respect. This capacity to apologize and assume responsibility signifies a shared esteem and investment in the relationship's welfare.

Commendation and Gratitude:

Expressions of gratitude fundamentally signify mutual respect. Acknowledging each other's positive attributes and contributions conveys appreciation, underscoring the value placed on the relationship.

Celebrating Triumphs

Marking each other's accomplishments showcases pride and respect. Celebratory recognition underscores respect for hard work and commitment, fortifying trust, and empathy.

ENRICHING YOUR PARTNERSHIP

As relationships mature, cultivating mutual respect emerges as a pivotal endeavor. While challenging, the attainment of mutual respect is attainable through strategic approaches.

The ensuing ten strategies foster mutual respect in your relationship:

Attentive Listening

Prioritize absorbing your partner's perspective by according their undivided attention. This underscores their significance and forges respect.

Kind Verbalization:

Employ your words with care, embracing kindness and compassion. Choose expressions that uplift and support, forsaking negativity.

Uninterrupted Dialogue

Demonstrate respect by allowing your partner to express themselves without interruption. This communicates your regard for their thoughts and viewpoints.

Validating Emotions

Strive to grasp your partner's emotions and viewpoint, validating their feelings even when agreement is elusive.

Pardoning and Seeking Pardon

Demonstrate accountability for your mistakes while extending forgiveness. Embrace compromise and shared resolutions.

Blame-Free Resolution

Channel energy into constructive communication rather than accusations. Conflict resolution over blame promotes mutual respect.

Shared Dreams Support

Uplift each other's aspirations through thick and thin, offering unwavering encouragement and support.

Embracing Gratefulness

Frequent gestures of gratitude convey respect and appreciation for contributions. Simple acts of acknowledgment nurture mutual esteem.

Unvarnished Honesty

Forge a foundation of trust through transparent and non-judgmental communication. Respect blossoms within sincere and open expressions.

Dignified and Respectful Treatment

Anchor mutual respect in your conduct and words, eschewing harm, or disrespect. Value each other's worth and identity.

Acknowledging the Prerequisite of Respect

Understanding the centrality of respect in relationships underscores its indispensable nature. By weaving these practices into your relationship's fabric, you establish a haven of mutual respect. This nurtures an atmosphere of safety, positivity, and unwavering support, where both individuals thrive within a culture of appreciation and esteem.

To my fellow men, let us recognize the depth of emotions and vulnerabilities that women carry. They are not impervious, but rather intricately delicate, deserving of our utmost respect. Their submissiveness is not a weakness to exploit, but a gift to be cherished. We must honor our roles as partners and co-creators in this journey, extending understanding and empathy.

Acknowledge your partner's imperfections while embracing your own. Strengthen your bond through open communication, mutual support, and a commitment to growth. Approach your relationship as a union of equals, devoid of arrogance or superiority. Aspire to treat your wife as the queen of your heart, nourishing her with love and appreciation.

May our actions reflect the recognition that women, like us, are human beings deserving of respect and tenderness. Let us cultivate enduring love, fostering an environment where both partners flourish. In this harmonious dance of emotions and connection, we shall find true contentment and happiness.

Married men, when you invest genuine care in your wife, your love for her can blossom anew each day. Consider gifting her quality perfume – her enticing scent could draw you closer. Delight in selecting beautiful dresses that enhance her appearance; this may help you remain captivated by her charm. Present her with premium body creams and contribute to enhancing her hair's beauty. These actions serve as defenses against potential distractions, often known as extramarital affairs. Your wife's allure may attract admirers, but remember, infidelity devastates marriages.

In moments when your wife is weary of cooking, take the initiative to prepare a meal yourself, sharing food nurtures your connection. Attend to your crying child without hesitation; comforting them reinforces your bond as a parent. If you come across your wife's undergarments in the bathroom, and she's too fatigued to clean them, take the initiative to do so. After all, she is your partner. Should her purse run empty, replenish it without waiting for her to ask. Never force her to beg for financial support. When her cooking doesn't suit your taste, address the matter with kindness and suggestions for improvement. Avoid belittling her in front of others; save correction for private moments. Strive to be consistent in character both at home and outside, ensuring your family cherishes your presence.

When you discover a remarkable woman, cherish, and safeguard her. Her submission is a sign of trust, not an opportunity for exploitation. Do not assume you can behave carelessly while she remains committed. Reject the notion of treating her solely as a sexual object or servant. Her unspoken concerns should trouble you; everyone has limits, and once she reaches hers, she might react strongly. Remember, women are humans with feelings, not mere playthings.

Respect her, treating her as royalty, and demonstrate that she holds the key to your heart. Occasionally assist her while cooking, as shared responsibilities strengthen your bond. Extend acts of care, such as assisting with chores she hasn't encountered before, like bathing. Engage in playful activities like pillow fights, making her feel cherished. Honesty and pride in her presence are crucial. Seduction, tidiness, and discretion in private matters are essential. Avoid discussing your private life with friends; handle situations maturely, trusting that God's guidance will prevail.

Acknowledge her feelings, reciprocating the respect you expect. Her reactions mirror the treatment she receives. Accept her imperfections, recognizing that personal growth is a mutual journey. Strive to address your own weaknesses, as lasting change stems from within. Do not use another person to fill the void left by an ex; choose a partner who has supported you through thick and thin. Reject the urge to abandon her when success alters your circumstances. Good intentions matter; approach relationships ethically. Remember, karma takes note of our actions. The quest for a quality partner is guided by divine grace. Men, nurture your relationship by demonstrating kindness and affection. Remember, women possess an inherent delicacy that endures despite age. Small gestures hold immense power in touching a woman's heart. Handle her with the tenderness due to a precious being. Dedicate time and attention to her needs, guarding against potential rivals. Protect your connection – the gap you leave might be the foothold for another. Embrace gratitude and contentment in what you share.

SIGNS OF MATURITY IN MARRIAGE

Here are some signs of maturity:

Handling Differences Gracefully

As a husband, displaying emotional maturity involves not refusing food due to anger after your wife has prepared it. Learn to address issues constructively without allowing unnecessary tension to build. While taking time to cool off is okay, avoid abandoning your home in anger.

Balanced Assertion of Authority

Recognize that even when your wife disobeys or disrespects you, constantly emphasizing your authority is unnecessary. True leadership is evident through actions and understanding, not through constant proclamation.

Communication and Conflict Resolution

Resorting to threats, abuse, or discussing marital problems with everyone hinders growth. Instead, address your wife's mistakes privately, correct, and communicate to resolve issues together.

Avoiding Malice and Public Ridicule

Keeping malice or publicly berating your wife doesn't lead to positive outcomes. Rise above such behaviors and display maturity by handling disagreements respectfully and privately.

Sharing Responsibilities

While a woman may manage the household as a full-time homemaker, lending a helping hand is a sign of a considerate partner. Participating in chores and expressing gratitude fosters a healthier environment.

Supporting and Encouraging

A true partner supports and encourages their spouse. Instead of merely comparing, assist with childcare tasks and show appreciation. Simple gestures like checking in during chores can make a significant difference.

Emotional Openness

He exhibits a fearlessness in expressing his emotions. In contrast to outdated notions of concealing vulnerability, a mature man readily shares his feelings. His emotional range extends beyond mere tears, anger, or frustration; he unveils his inner thoughts, elucidating the reasons behind his emotional state. This approach fosters transparency and reduces unnecessary drama. After all, how can solutions arise if issues remain unspoken?

Genuine Honesty

Honesty emerges as a hallmark of his maturity. No longer reliant on falsehoods or deceit to fulfill his desires, he engages with authenticity and meets your gaze with sincerity. His self-assuredness permits him to offer sincere love, contributing to the beauty and security of any relationship.

Harmony as Choice

Confronted by life's inevitable provocations, his response reflects a commitment to peace over conflict. Rather than engaging in fruitless battles or asserting dominance, he exercises discernment in his reactions. This emblem of maturity signifies his ability to selectively engage in disputes, valuing tranquility over empty victories.

Exemplary Patience

Patience stands as a virtue within his mature demeanor. Acknowledging life's imperfections and the inevitable deviations from even the most meticulous plans, he refrains from hasty reactions. This trait extends to interpersonal interactions, enabling him to approach misunderstandings with equanimity and understanding.

Adaptable Resilience

Immaturity begets rigidity, an aversion to change or alternative perspectives. In contrast, maturity shines through his willingness to embrace change and acknowledge life's impermanence. While his views may diverge from others, he remains receptive, abstaining from initiating debates and instead fostering an environment of respect for differing opinions.

Steadfast Resilience

Mature masculinity manifests in his resilience during trials and uncertainty. As a family leader, he exudes flexibility and optimism in the face of adversity. His composed demeanor prevails, offering solutions rather than succumbing to panic in overwhelming circumstances.

Realistic Optimism

The fusion of optimism and realism characterizes his mature outlook on life. Anticipating both positive and challenging experiences, he refrains from permitting negativity to tarnish his perspective. His mature approach involves meticulous evaluation of options and readiness to address problems effectively.

Receptive Mindset

Whereas immaturity resists correction, maturity embraces open-mindedness. The expansive nature of maturity enables the assimilation of diverse possibilities and ideas. Opinions transition from triggers to sources of growth, propelling his intellectual evolution and fostering a genuine appreciation for others' viewpoints.

Gratitude-Centered

The company of a mature man evokes a departure from perpetual complaints. Gratitude emerges as a defining trait, permeating his disposition. Whether grand or modest, his appreciation extends to the blessings of the present and the future, cultivating an enriching dynamic within the relationship.

Self-Acceptance Practitioner

Embracing himself unabridged is emblematic of his maturity. Casting aside the compulsion to conform for others' sake, he acknowledges his imperfections while embarking on a journey to actualize his best self. This practice nurtures growth and autonomy, anchoring his identity in authenticity.

Humility Embodiment

Maturity grants wisdom, enabling him to perceive the broader canvas of existence. This newfound awareness fuels his humility, dispelling any desire for undue attention. Recognizing equality as paramount, he positions himself as an inspirational force rather than the center of the universe, impervious to the intoxication of success, wealth, or intellect.

Accountability Maven

The realization of self-responsibility epitomizes maturity. He comprehends that his life's trajectory rests solely in his hands, eliminating the impulse to scapegoat others when plans falter.

Measured Self-Control

Heightened self-awareness empowers him with superior self-control. In lieu of instinctual reactions, he engages in thoughtful contemplation. His measured demeanor shines particularly in confrontational scenarios, where he opts for composure over confrontation.

Awareness and Detachment:

Anchored in self-awareness, a mature man transcends the trappings of trivial conflicts. Recognizing the futility of inconsequential disputes, he bypasses fruitless arguments, freeing his energy for more meaningful pursuits.

Respectful Paragon

Maturity begets respect, a quality he extends to all in his orbit. This respect manifests in his interactions with family, colleagues, and children, illustrating his evolution into a truly mature individual. When faced with the unexpected need to reschedule a date, a mature man's reaction contrasts starkly with that of his immature counterpart. His empathy and concern replace anger and toxicity, showcasing his growth and understanding that the world does not revolve solely around himself.

A HEALTHIER PERSPECTIVE

Society often reinforces outdated gender roles, suggesting that men should avoid tasks like washing clothes or cooking. It's time to challenge these perceptions. Men, you aren't limited to being providers; you can contribute to your household in meaningful ways.

If you're a man washing your clothes or cooking, don't be deterred by those who suggest you should only marry for domestic help. A fulfilling marriage involves shared responsibilities and mutual support.

Consider a mother advising her grown son to settle down solely for caretaking. Is this the true essence of partnership? Women face undue stress and fatigue due to these expectations. It's time to question the belief that men must avoid household tasks.

Men, who dictates that you must avoid chores? Break free from these stereotypes. Washing dishes, doing laundry, and making your bed aren't signs of weakness; they're signs of strength and equality in your relationship.

Marriage is not about seeking a maid but building a meaningful companionship. So, let's discard the notion that men require nurturing like children. Instead, embrace a genuine partnership where both contribute to a nurturing and supportive environment.

If you seek a partner for life, then seek a life partner. Yet, if matrimony beckons merely due to an aversion to household chores, then beckon a maid.

Cracking the Code to a Fulfilling Marriage

While weddings are filled with joy, the journey of marriage isn't always a walk in the park. Sometimes, it's more like an unexpected frosting explosion from the cake-cutting ceremony – well-intentioned, but not what you planned for. The truth is a happy marriage requires effort and understanding. Whether you're a newlywed or celebrating years together, we've consulted experts to unveil the secrets to a stronger, healthier, and yes, more blissful union.

▪ Embrace Disagreements

Even in the happiest marriages, disagreements are inevitable. It's important to note that all relationships experience ups and downs. The key is to listen to each other's viewpoints, recognize when things are going off track, and work together to mend the situation. Some of the happiest couples that we have met have weathered tough times. So, occasional arguments or rough patches don't necessarily signify an unhappy marriage; they're part of a normal relationship.

▪ Acknowledge Strengths

Happy marriages involve accepting your partner's strengths and weaknesses while setting realistic expectations. Instead of getting frustrated over minor annoyances, leverage each other's strengths. For instance, if you're better with numbers, manage the budget if your partner isn't as adept. This approach fosters well-being and relational satisfaction.

▪ Avoid Co-dependency

Contrary to famous line "You complete me," a healthy marriage is built on individuals who complement rather than complete each other. Maintaining personal interests, taking classes, and spending time with friends are vital to nurturing your own growth and happiness.

Share Experiences

While independence is essential, shared activities can strengthen your bond. Injecting new interests and hobbies into your relationship can create a deeper connection. Whether it's taking cooking classes or learning tennis together, these experiences enrich your connection and keep the relationship vibrant.

Cultivate Attraction

Attraction in a marriage is a choice you can make throughout your journey. Practicing "attraction thoughts" by focusing on your partner's appealing qualities, whether physical or emotional. A strong emotional connection often transcends physical appearance, emphasizing the importance of feeling connected to your spouse.

▪ Find Laughter Together

In the midst of life's challenges, maintaining humor can provide perspective and strengthen your bond. Couples in happy marriages often share inside jokes, send playful texts, or enjoy comedy together, fostering a deeper connection, as recommended by Morris.

▪ Practice Kindness

Respect and understanding are vital in a marriage. Avoid criticizing your partner's character during disagreements and instead express your needs with respect. Kindness is important in maintaining a happy marriage.

▪ Celebrate Small Victories

Acknowledging good times is as crucial as supporting each other during tough moments. Show gratitude and enthusiasm when your spouse shares positive news. By actively celebrating these moments, you reinforce the happiness in your marriage.

- **Express Appreciation**

Verbalize your appreciation daily. Recognize and compliment the thoughtful actions of your partner. This ongoing appreciation fosters a sense of value and prevents resentment from growing.

- **Embrace Change**

To sustain a happy marriage, be open to growth and adaptation. Our needs evolve, people change, and relationships mature. Bend and flex together, as to support each other's personal growth and the growth of your partnership.

In the dance of marriage, it's about being adaptable, respectful, and continually working together as a team to nurture a love that lasts a lifetime.

QUALITIES OF AN EXEMPLARY MAN

An exemplary man has the following qualities:

Loyalty

An authentic man upholds the sanctity of marriage and remains devoted to his partner. While many may stray, a true man remains faithful to one woman, honoring his marriage vows unwaveringly. Proverbs 20:6 highlights the rarity of a faithful man, setting him apart from those who lack this essential trait. Without loyalty, a man is akin to a mercenary.

Discipline

A story was once told of a man who simultaneously impregnated his wife, the house help, and his wife's younger sister. Such behavior lacks discipline and resembles that of a heedless goat. Proverbs 25:28 emphasizes the importance of self-control, comparing a lack of it to a city without walls, vulnerable and broken.

Humility

True leadership and power are accompanied by humility, fostering a partnership rather than an oppressive regime. A man devoid of humility dismisses corrections and disregards his partner's opinions. Even in scripture, righteous individuals led God to reconsider decisions. A man claiming immovability in his decisions mirrors dictatorship, not true masculinity.

Vision

Proverbs 29:18 emphasizes the significance of vision, revealing that without it, people perish. A genuine man possesses a clear life plan, including his role within a marriage. He acts with intentionality, carefully orchestrating his actions and endeavors. Unlike someone relying on luck, a visionary man knows what he wants, when, and how to attain it.

Spirituality

An exemplary man reveres and loves God, recognizing the divine's role in every facet of life – marriage, business, and personal pursuits. Devoid of spirituality, a man is devoid of substance.

UNDERSTANDING INTIMACY FOR MEN

Numerous men grapple with the concept of intimacy, influenced by societal norms that encourage them to project strength and control. This societal conditioning often hampers their capacity for authentic closeness, as genuine intimacy necessitates an embrace of vulnerability during connections with others.

What is Intimacy?

Intimacy entails a profound emotional connection. It transpires when two individuals can freely share their genuine emotions, thoughts, apprehensions, and aspirations. This level of sharing is achievable only when mutual trust is established, allowing both parties to take the courageous step of unveiling their vulnerabilities. Intimacy stands as a fundamental human need, as its absence often triggers feelings of solitude. In fact, a perceived absence of intimacy frequently ranks among the primary causes of relationship breakdowns.

Challenges Faced by Men

Men sometimes shy away from relationships and intimacy, fearing that they will forfeit their sense of self-reliance. Authentic emotional closeness is rooted in the art of balancing one's individuality while remaining interconnected with another.

It is common for men to conflate sexual activity with intimacy, when, in reality, the two are distinct. Intimacy can exist independently of physical encounters, and a sexual connection devoid of intimacy might prove unfulfilling. Conversely, when intimacy is present, sexual experiences can become deeply passionate and satisfying. Additionally, intimacy is not confined to the initial 'honeymoon' phase of a romantic relationship, characterized by heightened hormonal influences and intense desire. Beyond this phase, a relationship enters a new stage, demanding sustained effort from both partners to preserve the emotional closeness that once flowed effortlessly.

Moreover, a lack of an 'emotional vocabulary' might impede men from achieving intimacy. Men may perceive challenges in articulating their feelings, often feeling unease in conversations centered around emotions. It is essential to recognize that emotional expression is a skill that can be cultivated over time.

NURTURING INTIMACY

Acknowledge that developing intimacy is a learnable skill that demands practice. While it may seem daunting, don't let apprehension hinder your progress.

Genuine emotional closeness involves an inherent risk. Sharing your innermost self leaves you vulnerable to potential hurt if the other party responds unfavorably. However, extending trust often encourages reciprocation, fostering deeper connections.

Even if your thoughts and emotions are met with non-acceptance, your honesty can fortify the relationship. Learning to manage discomfort stemming from differing viewpoints without resorting to aggression or withdrawal is a valuable skill.

Pursuing intimacy is a personal journey, regardless of your partner's willingness to engage. Commence this endeavor whenever you're ready, as it's never too late.

Persistently maintaining emotional distance raises the likelihood of relationship deterioration. The potential harm from failing to open up is more significant than the discomfort of honesty.

Challenge stereotypes about masculinity, questioning notions like 'men must always be in control' or 'men shouldn't show vulnerability.' Seeking guidance from a counselor, whether individually or as a couple, is a constructive step toward enhancing intimacy.

Imperfection and complexity are inherent in any relationship. This reality remains evident even in the realm of fairy tales, where each character actively strives to nurture love's growth. While the initial experience of falling in love might be spontaneous, sustaining that euphoria demands concerted effort. Challenges are inevitable, and obstacles will undoubtedly emerge along the journey.

In essence, it is during these moments of hardship, when navigating difficulties as a team and weathering the inevitable bumps in the road, that true intimacy with a man is forged. Amidst uncertain circumstances, the potential to forge enduring and meaningful bonds with someone thrives. Mastering the art of cultivating intimacy within a marriage or relationship equips you with the tools to establish a connection that can withstand the tests of time, enduring for a lifetime.

The foundation of intimacy within your marriage can be compromised if you consistently arrive home late. Your wife's attraction to you isn't rooted in lavish gifts; it's nurtured by your ability to connect with her emotions. Building trust and faithfulness will magnify your appeal. Devoting time to your wife throughout the day is essential; expecting intimacy at night without prior connection might be unrealistic. Remember, women engage in lovemaking through emotional bonds; feeling loved is pivotal. Negative emotions can dampen her desire. If she's not in the mood, communicate and address concerns.

Respecting her today shapes your intimacy tomorrow. Understand that intimacy is an invitation, not a demand; it should be a shared celebration.

In summary, the struggle for intimacy is not uncommon among men due to societal influences, yet fostering genuine emotional closeness requires embracing vulnerability and dispelling myths about masculinity. Developing intimacy is a skill that demands effort, courage, and a willingness to challenge ingrained beliefs.

PLAYFULNESS IN MARRIAGE

A missing ingredient in many couples' lovemaking repertoire is a dash of fun and flirty playfulness. It's a mindset you're wanting to develop in your marriage–to naturally think in fun and flirty ways. If teasing, playfulness, and fun have not been a focus of your marriage, I encourage you to make it a priority and a personal area of expertise. The following are some specific ways to include more fun and flirty playfulness in your marriage—inside the bedroom and out:

Embracing playfulness with your spouse isn't contrary to faithfulness and marriage. Acknowledge your partner's sexual fantasies and make them a reality. Playfulness breathes life into your marriage, alleviating monotony. There are moments when your spouse craves not romance but playfulness. Being a devout believer doesn't exclude playfulness. It can manifest through actions like teasing, affectionate gestures, and flirtatious banter, even in the realm of online communication. Cultivate a private realm of playfulness between you two, creating lasting memories. Playfulness adds zest to your intimate life and keeps your relationship youthful. Marriage should be vibrant, not rigid. In your playfulness you can be naughty with your spouse.

It's Essential to Embrace naughtiness with Your Spouse".

1. Who better to naughty with than your spouse?
2. Marriage was never intended to be a dull routine.
3. Naughtiness enhances and nourishes the intimacy in your relationship.
4. We all possess a mischievous side; let it shine in your marriage.
5. Playfulness makes your spouse feel wanted, boosting their self-esteem, and reassuring them of your enduring attraction.
6. It creates cherished, unique memories.
7. Naughtiness ignites more passionate moments; it's a crucial part of foreplay.
8. Embracing naughtiness keeps both of you youthful and adds zest to your marriage.

9. Naughtiness deters your spouse from seeking excitement elsewhere. Don't settle for monotony.

10. Your spouse harbors fantasies, and it's your responsibility to explore them together.

11. Naughtiness sparks engaging conversations, leading to discussions beyond mundane tasks, finances, and household responsibilities.

EEFECT OF LACK OF PLAYFULNESS

Lack of playfulness can have significant consequence for relationships which includes:

Distrust

Nothing destroys play as much as distrust. The centerpiece of playfulness is opening oneself up to another for interaction. If we do not trust one another, we cannot be truly playful with one another. The importance of trust is one reason that playfulness is more of a presenting characteristic than the actual issue at play. The absence of playfulness is a symptom of a much deeper disease.

Weariness

Playfulness has the appearance of uselessness. While it is vital to the relationship, engaging in it can feel like a waste of time. If we are tired, we will not feel the freedom to be playful. We also will not have the energy and creativity necessary. Most couples I see remain playful in their marriage until they have their first child. When the weariness of pregnancy sets in, many lose their playfulness and are never able to regain it.

A Marital Rut

The relationship between playfulness and creativity is such that being in a rut can hinder both. As we repeat the daily routines over and over, we lose our sense of wonder, excitement, and joy. One of the first things to be lost is a happy playfulness between spouses.

While distrust, weariness and a marital rut can erode playfulness, we can also rediscover it. We can rebuild the habit into our relationships.

REBUILDING PLAYFULNESS

Playfulness is pertinent for productive unions. Here are some ways to rekindle playfulness in your marriage:

Restore Trust

This takes the most time, but true playfulness can't exist without it. A relationship is destined to die if it goes too long without trust. Thankfully, it can be rebuilt. By consistently being truthful, true to your word, and loving, trust can be restored. Many times, couples expect it to be rebuilt much faster than is realistic. I often tell people, you can't walk the wrong way for 10 years, turn around, and expect to be in the right place after walking 10 minutes. Trust can be built back faster than it was destroyed, but it takes longer than we like.

Rest

If trust is present, rebuilding playfulness becomes easy. Often the simplest task is to rest. As difficult as it is, find ways to give the best of your day to a spouse. It clearly can't happen every day because of work, children, and the demands of life, but if our spouses always get time with us at the end of the day when we are the most tired, it will be difficult to enjoy each other's company. On occasion, give your spouse your best. When you are most awake, most refreshed, most alive, give that time to the one you love the most.

Take Advantage of Shared Experiences

Playfulness is often built off of shared experiences. Inside jokes, stories only the two of you know, being able to link a current situation to a past experience can be vital to being playful. By having shared hobbies, learning something new together, or making sure you spend regular time together, we can build opportunities for fun to be experienced.

Change the Scenery

If a marital rut can erode playfulness, a change of scenery can quickly inject it back into a relationship. Even a crowded courtroom with shoplifters can be enough of a change of pace to allow playfulness to come forward. If a sense of play is missing in your relationship, when was the last time you took an extended trip with just your spouse? Sleep in, explore a new place, and watch how your conversation is different by being in a different place with different expectations and none of the demands of home.

Share Humor

Share funny videos or anecdotes to infuse light-heartedness and laughter into your relationship. Sharing jokes and humor can be an enjoyable way to connect.

Embrace Smile

Make a conscious effort to smile more at each other, promoting a lighter perspective on life's challenges. Small gestures like touching a furrowed brow can release tension and create playful moments.

Role Play

Engage in role-playing, simulate first dates, or act as if you're in the early stages of courtship to rekindle playful moments. Plan surprises for each other to add spontaneity and excitement.

Playfulness in the Bedroom

Within the bedroom, explore various forms of playful and flirty interactions. From undressing playfully to trying out bedroom games, experimenting with different scenarios can deepen intimacy and connection.

Send Fun and Flirty Texts to Each Other

Be sure to let your spouse know if you specifically want them to not read something sexual into it. Some spouses may need to overtly understand that flirty playfulness in their wife isn't necessarily a direct invitation to something more. The more a wife can experience giving and receiving teasing and playfulness without it leading to anything sexual, the easier it will be for her to continue to develop her playful side organically. Develop a repertoire of pet names or code words for sex or sexual things just between you to add that element of playfulness. It can also reduce discomfort and embarrassment about sexual things. Like the wife in the opening scenario, she referred to sex as "getting lucky." It could also be called "nooky" or "getting it on." Personal pet names like "baby doll," "honey bun," or "hot mama" give couples a chance to have a private language that includes sexual connotations that in time decrease the taboo nature of the subject itself.

Share Funny Video Clips/ Humorous Anecdotes

This will bring more light-heartedness and laughter into the relationship. Taking turns sharing the latest joke can be another fun way to laugh together.

Consciously Smile More at Each Other

This can help you both take life a little less seriously. It's a fun little tool for lightening the load of life.

Wink at Each Other

This is an amusing habit to get into as husband and wife. It's kind of fun to steal a wink across the room or to give a big, obvious wink just to be silly! One husband froze when he caught the eye of a woman winking at him suggestively. He didn't know what to do, until he turned and noticed the woman's husband behind him. He breathed a sigh of relief, then thought what a lucky guy that man was.

Surprise with Kind Unexpected Actions

Any kind of unexpected action has the potential for creating a playful moment. Whether it's a wife who unexpectedly goes up and kisses her husband's neck, or a husband who unexpectedly tells her wife how cute she is—these moments can add a bit of spice and put a smile on everyone's face.

Take Time Away

A great way to decrease focus on a particular outcome is to playfully plan on a completely different outcome than orgasm. This could be a session of naked cuddling with no intercourse allowed. It could be to do the kissing. It could be to plan to go to the park and make out somewhere, where intercourse is not even an option, to re-kindle the fun and enjoyment of just plain old making out!

Dynamize the Sex Experience

It might be fun to just be a little playful and silly about changing the whole sexual scenario. You might let your hair down during a sexual escapade like naked tickling matches, dancing naked, or just some intimate snuggling...unless you simply can't contain yourself!

Act out Scenes of the Past

After many years of marriage, it can be difficult to remember the fun and flirty times you had together in the beginning of your relationship. Why not role play a first date together? You could also role play as if you are in the beginning stages of courtship as you go about your daily lives. Perhaps there are some playful texts, emails, phone calls, random flowers you could send and receive. If this wasn't your forte back in your earlier days, now is a great opportunity to develop that playful side of yourself.

Play a Little Hard to Get

This is another great way to increase teasing and playfulness in your marriage. Talk about fun and flirty! One wife told me about her efforts to kiss or hug her husband when he got home from work. At first it was a bit of a drudgery to her, but then we suggested he play a little hard to get sometimes. When he started doing that, everything changed. It started to drive her crazy, in a good way. She went from it feeling like a duty to finding it a fun challenge to "get him" when he came home.

TIPS FOR IMPROVING PLAYFULLNESS

In the bedroom, there are all kinds of fun and flirty ways to tease and be playful with each other. You could undress each other playfully, teasing all along the way. You could play some peek-a-boo. You could do a striptease. You could play some of the fun bedroom games available out there. It's all about brainstorming ideas and identifying those that both of you are willing to try.

Playfulness in the bedroom has the added benefit of helping women close down the many mental windows open in their minds. Playing out a sexual scenario, for example, allows wives to engage themselves more fully in the lovemaking experience. Teasing them with tickling or non-sexual caressing helps them to be more present and more actively participate in the process of lovemaking.

Orchestrating surprises for each other increases spontaneity and playfulness. Oftentimes, one spouse has a greater preference for surprises and may even be better at pulling them off. There's something about setting up and receiving surprises that provide some fun stretching for the soul. It's can help us break free of needing to be in control or of having to follow a plan to be okay. Setting up a surprise getaway or just surprising your spouse with a night off to go and do whatever she wants are a couple of suggestions. It may be more difficult to willingly go with the surprise or spontaneous opportunity presented. It's something some may need to keep practicing.

One of my favorite fun ideas for couples is to create a "kissing closet" out of the kitchen pantry. It's a great way to be fun and flirty and to freak your kids out a bit as well. And who doesn't love doing that— especially if you have teenagers!

You might consider stealing a kiss in public every now and then. It will catch your sweetheart off guard at first and create some of that unexpected spice in your marriage. This is especially good homework for the spouse who tends to be more reserved. One wife decided she would kiss her husband in the movie theater at the end of every movie they saw. At first it was a little unnerving for her, but with a positive response from her husband, they've kept at. They've even gotten better at being playfully surreptitious about it. It is good for kids to see their parents loving each other, so a random appropriate kiss or hug in front of them is another fun and flirty idea to consider.

When either husband or wife must travel, it provides a perfect opportunity to tease and be playful with each other. Another favorite idea for travelling is to take your "Flat Spouse" with you. It's a full body cutout picture of your spouse, maybe even pasted onto cardboard that you take with you when you travel. You then take pictures of you and your Flat Spouse at various locations during your travels to send by phone or email back to your spouse at home.

If you forget to take your Flat Spouse, you could even just take some selfies with your cell phone and send them back home with a flirty text message.

Many couples often overlook the element of fun and playful interaction in their intimate relationship, which is a key ingredient missing from their lovemaking dynamic. Cultivating a mindset of light-heartedness and flirtatiousness can greatly enhance your marital bond. If your marriage has been lacking in teasing, playfulness, and fun, I strongly encourage you to prioritize and cultivate this aspect as a personal area of expertise. Below are specific strategies for infusing more playful and flirty dynamics into your relationship, both within and beyond the bedroom:

By addressing the factors that erode playfulness and implementing strategies to rebuild it, you can infuse your relationship with a renewed sense of fun, flirtatiousness, and intimacy. Remember that consistent effort and creativity are key to cultivating a playful and vibrant bond between partners.

CONCLUSION

A message to those who underestimate women. Dismissing the need for a woman? Think again!

Some men wrongly perceive women solely as objects of desire and sexual gratification. Considering women as mere symbols of sex reveals a misguided perspective. The purpose of marriage isn't based on such a limited view. A woman is a partner who complements your life's journey, propelling you towards greatness. Her role extends beyond being a spouse; she's your supporter, encourager, prayer partner, and a source of strength. A woman's influence can elevate your success and enrich your life. She aids in raising children, providing motherly love and support, contributing to a peaceful and joyful household. Embrace the idea of a companion, a confidant, and a lifelong friend. Recognize the divine intention behind this partnership. Acknowledging your need for a godly woman enhances your quest for fulfillment and happiness in marriage.

The true essence of the term "help meet"

One of the frequently misconstrued phrases in the Bible is the term "help meet" as found in the book of Genesis. Genesis 2:18 reads, "And the Lord God said, it is not good that the man should be alone; I will make him a help meet for him."

The interpretation commonly attributed to the term "help meet" suggests that Eve, unlike the other creatures of the Earth, was "suitable for" or "worthy" of Adam and was intended to be his companion and helper on Earth. While this interpretation carries merit, it falls short of fully encapsulating the profound and potent meaning embedded within the term "help meet." In its original Hebrew context, this term holds a significance far deeper than that of a mere "helper." By understanding the message that God conveyed to Adam, we gain a unique perspective on Eve's role and, more broadly, the role of women on this planet.

In Hebrew, the components of the term "help meet" originate from the words "ezer" and "k'enegdo." "Ezer," which is often translated as "help," encompasses a much richer implication. As Beverly Campbell expounds in her work "Eve and the Choice Made in Eden," biblical scholar David Freedman elucidates that the Hebrew word "ezer" is a fusion of two roots: one meaning "to rescue" or "to save," and the other denoting "strength." Over time, these roots coalesced into a single term, carrying the combined sense of salvation and strength. Initially signifying either "to save" or "to be strong," "ezer" eventually came to be understood as a blend of both meanings. Diana Webb, in "Forgotten Women of God," further clarifies this word by stating, "In eight of these instances the word means 'savior'. These examples are easy to identify because they are associated with other expressions of deliverance or saving." The term is most frequently employed to illustrate how God acts as an "ezer" to humanity.

For instance, the term "ebenezer" in 1 Samuel 7:12 underscores the power of God's deliverance, where "eben" signifies rock and "ezer" conveys "help" or "salvation." Consequently, "ebenezer" translates to "rock of help" or "rock of salvation." This identical "ezer" is the term God employed to describe Eve to Adam. Eve was not solely destined to be his helper or companion; she was intended to be his savior, his deliverer.

The other facet of "help meet" often interpreted as "meet for" or "fit for," is embodied in the word "k'enegdo." Unveiling the exact meaning of "k'enegdo" is somewhat elusive since it appears only once in the entire Bible. Diana Webb aptly explains, "Kenegdo could also mean 'in front of' or 'opposite.' This still didn't help much. Finally, I heard it explained as being 'exactly corresponding to,' like when you look at yourself in a mirror." Eve's purpose was not to be an exact replica of Adam. Instead, she was designed as his complementary counterpart, possessing attributes, responsibilities, and qualities that mirrored his lacking aspects. Analogous to their physical sexual organs being mirror opposites (one internal and the other external), their divine stewardships were meant to be opposite yet perfectly harmonious, fostering life. Eve emerged as Adam's spiritual equal, endowed with a vital saving power that was distinct from his.

Reflecting upon this profound insight into Eve's role and the equitable yet contrasting saving power she shares with Adam, it becomes evident that women are bestowed with a stewardship unique to them, one that parallels the significance of men's stewardship. By bringing forth and nurturing life, women serve as "saviors" to men, guiding them toward the light of Christ. Through the conception, creation, and bearing of mortal bodies, women facilitate the commencement of

God's children on their mortal journey, offering the prospect of perfection. Women serve as the gateway to this world, catalyzing progress, and exaltation. Furthermore, by exhibiting willingness to make sacrifices, even potentially giving their lives to bring forth children, women epitomize the true essence of charity. From a child's very first breath, they experience charity and unconditional love. This profound gift from a mother directs the child's attention towards God and Christ. Every woman, regardless of her capacity to give birth, assumes the role of a savior to humanity when she expresses love towards men and nurtures children, bringing them closer to Christ.

Even Adam, whose physical form did not stem from a daughter of Eve, was saved, and liberated by a woman. Through Mary, a woman, Jesus

Christ emerged to vanquish the shackles of death and sin, atoning for Adam's transgression. The absence of a woman to bear Christ's earthly form would have left humankind lost and forever fallen, rendering Adam's purpose on Earth meaningless. Mary's role acted as the conduit that made Christ's mission possible, her nurturing serving as the catalyst for his triumph. Although Eve did not directly give physical life to Adam, she essentially rescued him from spiritual demise by paving the path for the advent of the Savior and Redeemer into the world. Thus, through a woman, salvation—embodied in Christ—literally manifested on Earth.

This perspective on Eve resonates powerfully, challenging conventional narratives surrounding her and the roles of women. "Through imprecise translation, our understanding of the powerful words used originally to describe Eve's role have been diminished. As a result, our understanding of Mother Eve has also been diminished." Consider if all, irrespective of gender, were educated to comprehend Genesis 2:18 in a manner akin to the following: "It is not good that man should be alone. I will make him a companion of strength and power who possesses saving capabilities and stands as his equal."

Understanding the genuine essence of "help meet" at an earlier juncture would have substantially influenced our perception of my role and mission as a woman. This perspective unveils the marvelous stewardship the Lord has entrusted to women. Had we grasped the profound identity of women and their pivotal stewardship, we would have invested less time and energy in frustration over not possessing a man's stewardship. Evidently, authentic power emanates when men and women acknowledge their distinct endowments, capacities, and roles, collaborating as equal partners to foster mutual success. The unity of body, soul, and mind between genders propels God's work forward; an intertwined existence that underscores our interdependence on one another and our reliance on Christ.

Imagine a world where men and women genuinely apprehend this reality—how transformative that would be!

NOTES

NOTES

ABOUT THE AUTHOR

Rev Winston Peccoo is a gifted Evangelist and teacher of the word, he is a Pastor of the church of God in Jamaica. A relationship coach and a domestic violence counsellor. A husband, father, and a grandfather.

He is a graduate of Faith School of Theology with honors. He hosted a regular program on his Facebook live every Tuesday night entitled "Relationship Corner". Rev Peccoo has been walking with Jesus for 39 years and has preach and teach across denominations and are guide by his favorite passage of scripture found in Hebrew 10:35 "Cast not away therefore your confidence which hath great recompence of reward". His passion and desire are to see relationships grow and glow. He is a community activist and was recently awarded by the Area Three (3) arm of the Jamaica Constabulary Force (JCF) Clarendon Division for his passion, unconditional commitment, and enduring dedicated service. He has served and lead several school boards in St Catherine and Clarendon. He is a Justice of the Peace and is married to Dian Johnson an entrepreneur and managing director of DJ Professional and Paralegal Services. They reside in Frank field Clarendon.

NOTES

NOTES

Manufactured by Amazon.ca
Acheson, AB